THE SPOOKIEST
TRICKS & TREATS

JOKE
B**O**K

=EVER!=

Editors of Portable Press

PORTABLE
PRESS

San Diego, California

Portable Press
An imprint of Printers Row Publishing Group
10350 Barnes Canyon Road, Suite 100, San Diego, CA 92121
www.portablepress.com • mail@portablepress.com

Portable Press
Publisher: Peter Norton • Associate Publisher: Ana Parker
Senior Developmental Editor: April Farr
Developmental Editor: Vicki Jaeger
Project Editor: Kelly Larsen
Senior Product Manager: Kathryn C. Dalby
Production Team: Jonathan Lopes, Rusty von Dyl

Content curation: Patrick Merrell
Cover and interior concept: Patrick Merrell
Cover: Rosemary Rae
Interior: SunDried Penguin

Library of Congress Cataloging-in-Publication Data

Title: The spookiest tricks & treats joke book ever! / editors of Portable Press.
Description: San Diego, CA : Printers Row Publishing Group, 2019. |
    Audience: Ages 6+ | Audience: Grades K-3.
Identifiers: LCCN 2019006189 | ISBN 9781684129416 (book/trade paper)
Subjects: LCSH: Halloween--Juvenile humor. | Wit and humor, Juvenile.
Classification: LCC PN6231.H547 S66 2019 | DDC 818/.60208--dc23
LC record available at https://lccn.loc.gov/2019006189

ISBN: 978-1-68412-941-6

Printed in the United States of America

24 23 22 21 20   2 3 4 5 6

What did the art critics call Frankenstein's monster's painting?

A monsterpiece.

When are ghosts the noisiest?

In the moaning (morning).

1

Why do demons and ghouls get along so well?

Because demons are a ghoul's best friend.

What did the ghoul say after he dug three holes in the ground?

"Well, well, well!"

4

**What do you get if you cross
a ghoul with a collie?**

A dog that eats you and
then runs for help.

Ghoul: I don't trust gnomes.

Goblin: Why not?

**Ghoul: Their brains are too near
their butts.**

**Where can you find ghouls
on weekends?**

On ghoul-f courses.

**What was the sea monster's
favorite TV show?**

Whale of Fortune.

How do you keep an ogre from smelling?

Plug up his nose.

What did the one-armed ogre have in common with his broken watch?

He didn't have a second hand.

What do ghouls eat in Europe?

Hungarian ghoulash.

What kind of makeup does a ghoul put on?

Mas-scare-a.

GALLONS OF GHOULS

Why did the ghoul eat a lamp?

He wanted a light meal.

What was the ghoul doing at the dinner table?

Goblin her food.

What happened to the flowers in the ghoul's garden?

They grue-some.

What do ghouls put on hot dogs?

Ghoulden's Mustard.

What should you do when five ghouls
show up at your front door?

Hope it's Halloween!

Why do ghouls eat only organic food?

Because it's super natural.

When did most ghouls come
to California?

During the Ghould Rush.

What's a ghoul's favorite cereal?

Scream of Wheat.

What Shakespearean play did the goblins like best?

Romeo and Ghouliet.

How do ogres keep their feet dry?

They wear ghoul-oshes.

What is a ghoul's favorite movie?

Goon with the Wind.

How does Shrek like his eggs?

Ogre easy.

Head ogre: Use "worm eye" in a sentence.

Little ghoul: Where worm eye parents born?

Head ogre: Can you use "ape" and "eel" in a sentence?

Little ghoul: You need to take ape eel (a peel) off a banana to eat it.

What did the goblins serve at their Halloween party?

Ghoulade.

What position did the goblin play on the hockey team?

Ghoulie.

How do you know if an ogre is hungry?

He's breathing.

**Why did the giant wear
purple suspenders?**

Because his red ones broke.

Knock-knock!
Who's there?
Thumb.
Thumb who?
Thumb-one's right behind you!

**What do you get when a creepy
creature goes to the bathroom?**

Cree-pee.

Why are ghouls forgetful?

Because everything goes in one ear and out three others.

When does an ogre have to go to the dentist?

Tooth-hurty (2:30).

What steps should you take when an ogre is chasing you?

Very big ones.

What would you call a kindhearted ogre?

A failure.

Who did the ogre go to the dance with?

His girl-fiend.

Why did the ghoul eat her homework?

Because the teacher told her
it was a piece of cake.

**What did the ghoul's left eye say
to his right eye?**

"Between us, something smells."

What kind of ghoul keeps good time?

A metro-gnome.

What did the goblins sell door-to-door?

Ghoul Scout cookies.

**What's the best thing about
being an ugly ogre?**

You don't need to buy a costume
for Halloween.

Little ogre: I hate my teacher.

Mother ogre: Then just eat your salad.

**Mother ghoul: Boris, what did your
father say when you ate the dog?**

Boris: Should I leave out the
bad words?

Mother: Yes, please.

Boris: He didn't say anything.

Why did the ghoul say, "Moo! Moo!"?

She was studying a foreign language.

How can you tell when an ogre is full?

When he doesn't try to eat you.

If a red goblin is red and looks like a goblin, what is a purple goblin?

A red goblin in disguise.

Try saying this three times quickly:

"The ghoul's gruel grew cool."

Ghoul (on the phone): Doctor, my son swallowed a pen.

Witch doctor: Bring him to see me in the morning.

Ghoul: What should I do until then?

Witch doctor: Use a pencil.

How do you fit three ogres in a refrigerator?

Take out one dragon.

What does a goblin become after she's five days old?

Six days old.

2

TRICK OR TREAT!

What do Twitter users say to one another on Halloween?

"Trick or tweet?"

Why is Halloween good for your health?

The more times you celebrate it, the longer you live.

What's the scariest day of the week?

Frightday.

What do hockey players say
on Halloween?

"Hat trick or treat?"

What do you get if you combine
Halloween and St. Patrick's Day?

Patrick-or-treaters.

What do you call a hot dog
with nothing in it?

A hollow-weenie.

Why was 6 afraid of 7?

Because 7, 8, 9 (7 ate 9).

What kind of rope is the scariest?

Afraid (a frayed) one.

How do you write a book about Halloween?

Hire a ghost writer.

What's long and green and lies lifelessly around the yard?

A garden hose.

Knock-knock!
Who's there?
Hal.
Hal who?
Halloween!

Knock-knock!
Who's there?
Phillip.
Phillip who?
Phillip my bag with candy, please!

Knock-knock!
Who's there?
Orange.
Orange who?
Orange you glad it's Halloween?

TRICK OR TREAT!

Knock-knock.
Who's there?
Figs.
Figs who?
Figs your doorbell, it's broken!

Knock-knock!
Who's there?
Abbott.
Abbott who?
Abbott time you answered your door.

Knock-knock!
Who's there?
Disguise.
Disguise who?
Disguise dressed up like a monster.

21

TRICK OR TREAT!

Knock-knock!
Who's there?
Police.
Police who?
Police give me some candy.

Knock-knock!
Who's there?
Candy.
Candy who?
Candy cow jump over the moon?

Knock-knock!
Who's there?
You.
You who?
**"Yoo-hoo" back at you.
Nice to see you.**

Knock-knock!
Who's there?
Hatch.
Hatch who?
Gesundheit!

Knock-knock!
Who's there?
Lettuce.
Lettuce who?
Lettuce in, it's freezing out here.

Knock-knock!
Who's there?
Ya.
Ya who?
You sound pretty excited to see me.

Knock-knock!
Who's there?
Ken.
Ken who?
Ken I have some more candy?

Knock-knock!
Who's there?
Horton hears a
Horton hears a who?
Oh, you like Dr. Seuss too.

Knock-knock!
Who's there?
Robin.
Robin who?
**Robin you—
hand over all your candy.**

TRICK OR TREAT!

Knock-knock!
Who's there?
Howl.
Howl who?
Howl you know if you don't open the door?

Knock-knock!
Who's there?
Luke.
Luke who?
Luke through the peephole and you'll see.

Knock-knock!
Who's there?
Says.
Says who?
Says me, that's who!

Why did the skunk bring toilet paper to the Halloween party?

Because it was a party pooper.

What happened when the Invisible Man was invited to the party?

He didn't show up.

When do monsters like to party the most?

April Ghoul's Day.

What happens when werewolves get together for a party?

They have a howling good time.

What's the best food to roast over
a fire at the Halloween party?

Hallow-weenies.

What do you call a bug that falls in
a bottle of apple cider?

An insider (in cider).

If you send Bob out to buy four apples
on Halloween, what should you
say to him?

"Bob, four apples" (bob for apples).

What do aliens use to buy
Halloween candy?

Starbucks.

How much does it cost a pirate to get his ears pierced?

A buck an ear (buccaneer).

Why did the pirate's parrot cross the road?

It didn't. It stayed on the shoulder.

Why is Superman's costume so tight?

Because he wears a size "S."

Why couldn't the kid in the pirate costume see the movie?

Because it was rated arrrrr.

What kind of pet did Aladdin have?

A flying car-pet.

What are you if you call
the Big Bad Wolf a jerk?

Little Rude Riding Hood.

What do you call a smart genie?

A genie-us.

When is a piece of wood like a queen?

When it's a ruler.

Why was the Little Mermaid riding a seahorse?

She was playing water polo.

What did the sea say to the mermaid?

Nothing. It just waved.

How come Jack always knows what's going on in the garden?

Because Jack and the beans talk.

Where do kings and queens get crowned?

On their heads.

Why did Robin Hood steal from
the rich?

Because the poor didn't have anything
to steal.

Girl: What do you want to be
for Halloween?

Boy: I want to be full of candy.

What kind of candy is never on time?

Choco-late.

What do you call a sheep dipped
in chocolate?

A candy baa.

3

What did the pirate wear over
his eye on Halloween?

A pumpkin patch.

I was wondering why the pumpkin kept
getting bigger and bigger...

...then it hit me!

Knock-knock!
Who's there?
Orange.
Orange who?
"Orange you glad it's me?"

**What is a pumpkin's favorite
street corner?**

Hollywood and Vine.

**How was the pumpkin feeling
before being picked?**

Vine, thank you.

What are gourds afraid of?

Things that go pumpkin the night.

PUMPKIN FUN

What do you call a pumpkin that's been dropped off a cliff?

Squash.

What's orange and can leap tall buildings in a single bound?

Super Pumpkin.

What do pumpkins use to pay for things?

Pumpkin bread.

Why can't pumpkins keep secrets on Halloween?

Because they're always spilling their guts.

PUMPKIN FUN

What do you call a pretty pumpkin?

Gourd-geous.

If you get pumpkins from pumpkin vines, where do you get eggs from?

Eggplants.

Who helps pumpkins to cross streets?

Crossing gourds.

What's black, white, and orange, and waddles?

A penguin carrying a pumpkin.

PUMPKIN FUN

What are the funniest pumpkins?

Joke-o'-lanterns.

Why didn't the coach of Cinderella's baseball team say anything?

Because her coach was a pumpkin.

Why did the elephant paint its toenails orange?

To hide in a pumpkin patch.

What do you call a gourd's family members?

Pump-kin.

Where's the best place to put
a pumpkin pie?

In your belly.

Who's the leader of all the pumpkins?

The pump-king.

Why did the pumpkin turn red when it
was put in the refrigerator?

It saw the salad dressing.

Try saying this three times fast:

"Pumpkin pie spice."

**Why was the jack-o'-lantern afraid
to cross the road?**

It had no guts.

**What should a pumpkin never say
to a person with a knife?**

"Cut it out."

What do you call a really big pumpkin?

A plumpkin.

**Why are candles put inside
jack-o'-lanterns?**

Because it's hard to put
them underneath.

**What did the pumpkin say
to the gourd?**

Nothing, pumpkins can't talk.

**Who led the pumpkins to
the grocery store?**

The pie piper.

**What do you say to someone carving
a jack-o'-lantern?**

"Happy hollowing!"

**What rock band is bad to listen
to on Halloween?**

Smashing Pumpkins.

PUMPKIN FUN

What's orange and goes *putt-putt-putt*?

An outboard pumpkin.

**What's orange and sounds like
a bumpkin?**

A pumpkin.

**What do you call it when a pumpkin
goes snorkeling?**

A seedy dive.

**What do you call a carved pumpkin
made of wood?**

A lumberjack-o'-lantern.

What do you call a hollowed-out
pumpkin filled with candy-coated
popcorn, peanuts, and a prize?

Cracker jack-o'-lantern.

What do Las Vegas casinos put by their
front doors for Halloween?

Jackpot-o'-lanterns.

How can you tell if a
jack-o'-lantern is angry?

It's burning inside.

Weird but true: years ago,
turnips were used as jack-o'-lanterns
in Scotland and Ireland!

What do you get if you divide
the circumference of a
jack-o'-lantern by its diameter?

Pumpkin pi.

How do pumpkins reach high places?

They use jack-o'-ladders.

What did the orange pumpkin say
to the green pumpkin?

"Why orange you orange?"

Why do pumpkins sit outside people's
doors on Halloween?

Because they have no legs
to get up and leave.

What do you call a stolen pumpkin?

Hijack-o'-lantern.

**What did one pumpkin say
to the other?**

"You glow, girl!"

**What do you call a really
annoying pumpkin?**

Jerk-o'-lantern.

**What did the cow leave in the field
after eating a pumpkin?**

Pumpkin pies.

What's small and furry with enormous cheeks?

A chipmunk eating two pumpkins.

Why did the pumpkin go out with a prune?

Because it couldn't get a date.

What musical instrument is a pumpkin's favorite?

The a-gourd-ion (accordion).

What part of a pumpkin is really good at math and science?

The STEM.

4

What did the vampire farmer put on top of his barn?

A weather vein.

What did the monsters call Count Dracula after a witch turned him into a goose?

Count Down.

45

What is the one test the vampire passed in school?

His blood test.

Where do vampires stay when they're in the hospital?

The bat wing.

What does a vampire never have for dinner?

Stake.

Why can't you believe a vampire when he's in his coffin?

He lies.

What do you call it when two vampires reach a victim at the same time?

A necktie.

What does a vampire call out when he's done sucking a victim's blood?

"Necks!"

What is Dracula's favorite superhero?

Batman.

How can you tell if a vampire is crazy?

He has bats in his belfry.

What goes *chomp, chomp,* "ouch"?

A vampire with a sore fang.

Why did Dracula's girlfriend leave him?

He was a pain in the neck.

How did the angry villagers track down Dracula?

They used bloodhounds.

How can you tell if a vampire has raided your refrigerator?

There are two tiny holes in your can of tomato juice.

**How can you tell if
a vampire has a cold?**

If he's coffin.

What did Dracula put in his flashlight?

Bat-teries.

**Where does Dracula like to
go on vacation?**

The Red Sea.

**What did Dracula's son do for
the baseball team?**

He was the bat boy.

DEAD AHEAD

**What did Dracula's daughter do
for the baseball team?**

She was the home plate vampire.

**What does Dracula do when he
gets tired of working?**

He takes a coffin break.

Why did Dracula reject his blind date?

She wasn't his blood type.

Why wasn't Dracula in his coffin?

He got up to go to the batroom.

Where did Dracula go when he visited New York City?

The Vampire State Building.

Why did the vampire bury the trophy?

He wanted it engraved.

Who likes vampires?

Their fang clubs.

If a black cat brings bad luck, what does a vampire bring?

Bat luck.

Where was the hypnotist vampire born?

Trance-ylvania.

What does Dracula put on his mashed potatoes?

Grave-y.

What is a vampire's favorite Halloween treat?

A sucker.

What is a vampire's favorite holiday?

Fangsgiving.

Why did the vampire join the circus?

He wanted to be an acro-bat.

What did the vampire say to his victim?

"Nice gnawing you."

**What do you call a vampire
with asthma?**

Vlad the Inhaler.

Why are vampires like false teeth?

They come out at night.

What do you get if you cross a cooking utensil with a vampire?

Count Spatula.

Why did the little zombies stay away from Dracula?

He was a bat influence.

What do polite vampires say after sucking someone's blood?

"Fang you very much."

What is a vampire's favorite victim?

A person with high blood pressure.

DEAD AHEAD

**What two TV shows were
the vampire's favorites?**

The Bat-chelor and *The Bat-chelorette*.

What is a vampire's favorite sport?

Casketball.

What's blue and has fangs?

Dracula holding his breath.

Which *Star Wars* movie was Dracula in?

The Vampire Strikes Back.

What do you get if you cross a teacher with a vampire?

Lots of blood tests.

What song do vampires hate?

"You Are My Sunshine."

What do you call a vampire 200 miles from home?

A cab.

Where does Dracula wash his clothes?

In a bat tub.

What honor was Dracula awarded in his high school yearbook?

Most likely to suck-ceed.

What happened when Dracula tried to suck blood from a zombie?

He bit the dust.

What did Dracula say about his girlfriend?

"It was love at first bite."

Why didn't the zombie eat animals?

Because she was a people person.

5

HAUNTED HILARITY

What do you call a special guest at a haunted house?

The ghost of honor.

What happens when ghosts haunt a theater?

The actors get stage fright.

What do you say to a quiet ghost?

"Come on, spook up!"

What is a ghost's favorite dessert?

Ice scream.

**What's a ghost's favorite
amusement park ride?**

The roller ghoster.

**What is a ghost's second-favorite
amusement park ride?**

The scary-go-round.

What did one ghost say to the other?

"Do you believe in people?"

What was the ghosts' favorite party game?

Hide-and-shriek.

What do you call it when ghosts make mistakes?

Boo-boos.

Which ghost is the best dancer?

The boogie man.

What did the man say when identifying the ghost that attacked him?

"That's the spirit!"

What did the mother ghost say to her kids in the car?

"Fasten your sheetbelts."

Why do ghosts like an elevator?

It raises their spirits.

Why do ghosts wail and moan on cold nights?

You would too if all you had on was a sheet.

What is it called when ghosts
play hide-and-seek?

Peek-a-boo.

What do Australian ghosts like to throw?

Boo-merangs.

Where do baby ghosts go during
the day?

Dayscare centers.

What do you find in a ghost's nose?

Boo-gers.

**Why did the policeman give
a ticket to the ghost?**

He didn't have a haunting license.

What is a ghost's favorite dessert?

Booberry pie.

**Why don't ghosts like rain
on Halloween?**

It dampens their spirits.

What is a ghost's favorite song?

"Pop Ghost the Weasel."

HAUNTED HILARITY

What did the woman say when ghosts moved in next door?

"There ghost the neighborhood."

What kind of shirts do ghosts wear?

Boo-tees.

Do ghosts have fun at parties?

Yes, they have a wail of a time.

Why did the ghost starch her sheet?

She wanted everyone to
be scared stiff.

What did the baby ghost call his mother or his father?

Transparent.

How did the ghost learn to play the piano?

By using sheet music.

What is a ghost's favorite dinosaur?

A terror-dactyl.

How do ghosts stay fit?

They exorcise daily.

When does a ghost's workweek start?

On Moan-day.

What do you call the ghost of a chicken?

A poultry-geist.

**What's a ghost's favorite thing
to do at a hoedown?**

Scare dancing.

Who styles a ghost's hair?

A bootician.

What does a bootician use to style a ghost's hair?

A scare dryer.

What did the little ghost eat for lunch?

A booloney sandwich.

Where do ghosts mail their letters?

At the ghost office.

What did the ghost teacher say to her class?

"Watch the board and I'll go through it again."

**Who speaks at a ghost
press conference?**

A spooksperson.

Try saying this three times quickly:

"Guest ghosts guess close."

What was the ghost's favorite dinner?

Spook-ghetti and meatballs.

**What do you get if you cross a cocker
spaniel, a poodle, and a ghost?**

A cocker-poodle-boo.

**What do baby ghosts wear
on their feet?**

Boo-ties.

**What did the ghost win at
the talent contest?**

The boo-by prize.

Where did the ghost go on vacation?

The Boo-hamas.

**What did the teacher say to
the misbehaving ghost?**

"Ghost stand in the corner."

6

What did the monster do when she lost one of her hands?

She looked in her handbag for another.

What do you do if a monster rolls his eyes at you?

Pick the eyes up and roll them back.

Why did the long-snouted monster eat his aunt?

Because he was an anteater.

What do monsters love to eat for dessert?

Devil's food cake.

What's the best way to talk to a monster?

Long distance.

Why did the bog monster rarely go out?

He was swamped.

What's the worst way to find a monster?

On the loose.

What happened when the fog monster left town?

He was mist.

Why did the grandmother monster knit three socks for Halloween?

She heard her granddaughter grew another foot that year.

Why don't monsters eat candy with their fingers?

It tastes much better to eat fingers separately.

How do you keep an ugly monster in suspense?

I'll tell you later.

What do little monsters call their parents?

Mummy and deady.

What is the smartest monster?

Frank-Einstein.

What should you say if you see a two-headed monster?

"Bye, bye!"

What kind of monster has two noses and two mouths?

One with two heads.

What kind of monster has the best hearing?

The eeriest (ear-iest) one!

Where do monsters shop for food?

The gross-ery store.

How do monsters find out what's in their future?

By reading the horror-scope.

**How do you keep a monster
from biting his nails?**

Give him a box of screws.

**Why did the monster move out of
the neighborhood?**

She was fed up with her neighbors.

**Why did the monster turn
into a human?**

Because you are what you eat.

**She: The police are looking for a
monster with one eye called Bertha.**

He: What's the other eye called?

He: What do you call a 12-foot monster with 57 teeth?

She: Sir or madam!

Why were the two cyclops monsters always fighting?

They couldn't see eye to eye.

Why did the monsters climb up on the roof at dinnertime?

They heard all meals were on the house.

Did you hear the joke about the monster's fart?

It's a gas.

What has 40 legs, 40 arms, and sings?

A school choir.

What has one horn and flies?

A garbage truck.

Which hand do monsters usually write with?

Neither, they usually write with pencils.

What's ugly, green, and has wheels?

A monster...I lied about the wheels.

Why did the monster fall asleep on the bicycle?

Because it was two tired.

What do you call a monster after he dies?

A nonster.

What monster plays tricks on Halloween?

Prank-enstein.

What time is it when the clock strikes 13?

Time to get the clock fixed.

Where should a 500-pound monster go?

On a diet.

**What do you do with a smelly,
green monster?**

Throw it out and get a fresher
one at the store.

What do little monsters like to slurp up?

Alpha-bat soup.

**What can go in a monster's cave, stay
five hours, and come out alive?**

A monster.

Knock-knock!

Who's there?

Iran.

Iran who?

Iran away from the monster.

Why did Frankenstein's monster hold his bride tight?

Because he had a crush on her.

Why did the monster tiptoe past the camping store?

He didn't want to wake the sleeping bags.

What do you get if a huge, hairy monster steps on Batman and Robin?

Flatman and Ribbon.

What aftershave do monsters use?

Brute.

Waiter on an ocean liner: Would you like to see the menu?

Monster: No thanks, just bring me the passenger list.

What happened to Ray when he ran into the monster?

He became ex-Ray.

What do monsters call garbage cans?

Dinner plates.

Monster salesman: Ma'am, this book will help your husband get ahead.

Monster wife: Thanks, but he's already got two.

What's the hardest part of making monster soup?

Stirring in the monsters.

How did Frankenstein's monster keep himself charged when roaming the countryside?

Lightning bugs.

7

IT'S MAGIC!

What keeps witches warm in the winter?

Hot spells.

What do you call witches when they go to the beach?

Sand witches.

83

**What do you call a witch
who's not green?**

III.

How does a witch's cat get ahead?

It claws its way to the top.

Why do witches use brooms to fly?

Because the cords on vacuum
cleaners aren't long enough.

Why did the witch fail in school?

She couldn't spell.

**Who did the witch go to see
when she got sick?**

The witch doctor.

**Witch: You never take me
out anymore.**

Warlock: What's the use, you
keep coming back.

**What does a witch put on her door
to keep out burglars?**

A war-lock.

**What do you call tests in
wizardry school?**

Hex-aminations.

Why did the witch take her cat to the beach?

She wanted to see sandy claws.

Why did the witch's black cat throw up?

She was broom sick.

How many black cats can sit on an empty witch's broom?

Only one. After that, the broom isn't empty anymore.

What's worse than being a five-ton witch on Halloween?

Being her broom!

What did the nervous witch break out in?

Worry warts.

Why did the witch make her bowl of stew fly around the room?

She wanted some fast food.

Why did the witch's cat do everything the witch did?

She was a copy cat.

What did the witch drink to make herself beautiful?

Gore juice (gorgeous).

Why do witches wash their clothes in Tide?

Because it's too cold to do it out-tide.

What did the 50-foot rat say to the witch's cat?

"Here, kitty, kitty, kitty."

Warlock: I'm thirsty, can you make me a lemonade?

Witch: Poof! You're a lemonade.

What did the witch get when she turned her cat into a piece of wood?

A catalog.

What did the angry witch do while riding her broom?

She flew off the handle.

How do you make a witch scratch herself?

Take away her *w*.

Why doesn't a witch wear a flat hat?

Because there's no point to it.

Knock-knock!
Who's there?
Witches.
Witches who?
Witches the way to the haunted house?

What's old and ugly and has four wheels?

A witch on a skateboard.

What's the difference between a witch and the letters *m*, *a*, *k*, *e*, and *s*?

One makes spells, the other spells "makes."

Knock-knock!

Who's there?

Witch.

Witch who?

Witch one of you can fix my broom?

What do witches ask for at hotels?

Broom service.

IT'S MAGIC!

Knock-knock!
Who's there?
Wanda.
Wanda who?
Wanda go for a ride on my broom?

**What did the witch do when
her broom broke?**

She witch-hiked.

**What did the little witch want
for her birthday?**

A haunted dollhouse.

IT'S MAGIC!

What sound did the gas-powered witch's broom make?

Brrrroooom, brrrrooooommmm.

What do you call a witch's garage?

A broom closet.

Why did the witch take her broom through the car wash?

She wanted a clean sweep.

What sound does witch cereal make?

Snap, cackle, pop.

What is an evil candle called in California?

The wicked wick of the west.

What has green, warty skin, dresses in black, and goes round and round?

A witch who's stuck in a revolving door.

Why did the witch give up fortune-telling?

She saw no future in it.

What has six legs and flies?

A witch and her cat on a broom.

Will a witch hurt you if you run away?

It depends on how fast you run.

What's the best way to talk to a witch?

By telephone.

Why do witches get lots of good bargains?

Because they're good at hag-gling.

What does a witch sing at Christmas?

"Deck the halls with poison ivy..."

8

CREEPY CRITTERS

What did the spider do on the computer?

It created a website.

What has eight legs and goes undercover?

A spy-der.

What do spiders do after eating corn?

They spin cob-webs.

What are spiderwebs good for?

Spiders.

**What did the spider say to
the pesky fly?**

"Buzz off."

**What do you call a spider with
only four legs?**

Lefty lefty lefty lefty.

What kind of doctors are like spiders?

Spin doctors.

Why did the spider put ketchup on the fly before eating it?

It was out of mustard.

Why did the witch's spider keep getting loose?

The leash was too loose.

Why did the fly fly?

Because the spider spied her.

Why do people yell, "Spiiiiiiiiider!"

Because it has eight eyes (i's).

What happened when the man bit into a sandwich with a daddy longlegs in it?

It became a daddy shortlegs.

Why do spiders make good baseball players?

They know how to catch flies.

What do spiders order in French restaurants?

French flies.

Why do spiders spin webs?

Because they can't knit.

What is a spider's favorite day?

Flyday.

What did the spider say to the fly on Halloween?

"This web is my trick and you're my treat."

What do you call the second *Spider-Man* movie?

A spinoff.

What did the spider say when its web broke?

"Darn it!"

What is a spider's favorite beverage?

Apple spider.

What do you do when a tarantula gets out of its cage?

Walk carefully.

What do you call a nervous toad?

A worry wart.

What's worse than finding a worm in your spaghetti?

Finding half a worm in it.

What is a shark's favorite sandwich?

Peanut butter and jellyfish.

What is a killer whale's favorite meal?

A submarine sandwich.

What is the best shark repellent in the world?

The Sahara Desert.

What do you call worms with no teeth?

Gummy worms.

What do you find in a black-eyed cat's litter box?

Black-eyed pee.

If cars run on gas, what do black cats run on?

Their paws.

What sound does a bat's doorbell make?

Ding-dung.

What looks like half a black cat?

The other half.

Try saying this three times quickly:

"Black cat bath mats."

What is a black cat's favorite color?

Purr-ple.

What's a black cat's favorite orchestra section?

Purr-cussion.

In what way are cats like coins?

Heads on one side, tails on the other.

What's noisier than a hissing black cat?

Two hissing black cats.

What's noisier than two hissing black cats?

Two hissing black cats with megaphones.

What do black cats keep in the freezer?

Mice trays.

What does a cat use to smell good?

Purr-fume.

What do you call a destructive dinosaur?

Tyrannosaurus wrecks.

Man: What's that crocodile doing in my swimming pool?

Pool cleaner: I think it's the backstroke, sir.

What do you get if you cross a goose with a stampeding rhino?

An animal that honks before running you over.

Why are crocodiles bad dancers?

Because they have two left feet.

How do dinosaurs pay their bills?

With Tyrannosaurus checks.

Where do sharks go on vacation?

Finland.

What do termites eat for dessert?

Toothpicks.

Where do you go to replace a rat's tail?

A re-tail store.

106

9

CREATURE FEATURES

**What's hairy, has fangs,
and is four feet tall?**

An eight-foot-tall werewolf bending
over to tie his shoes.

**What happened when the werewolf
swallowed the clock?**

He got ticks.

Little boy: Mommy, everybody says I look like a werewolf.

Mother: Be quiet and comb your face!

What's hairy, has fangs, and can run faster than a locomotive?

Super Wolfman.

Where do werewolves live?

In werehouses.

What do you say if you spot a werewolf?

"There wolf!"

Who did the three werewolves find sleeping in Baby Werewolf's bed?

Ghoul-dilocks.

What's the best way to avoid an infection from werewolf bites?

Don't bite any werewolves.

What kind of Halloween creatures can be put in the washing machine?

Wash-and-wear wolves.

Monster: Where do fleas go in the winter?

Werewolf: Search me.

What do you call a werewolf you don't know?

A whowolf.

What do you get if you cross a werewolf and a menace?

A fur-nace.

What did one werewolf say to the other?

"Howl's it going?"

What do you get if you cross a werewolf with a cat?

You have to get a new cat.

What did the cowboy say after the Wolfman ate his dog?

"Well, dog-gone!"

How do you stop a werewolf from attacking you?

Throw a stick and yell "fetch!"

What do you say to a backward werewolf?

"Flower, ew!" (because that's "werewolf" spelled backward).

What does Bigfoot eat for lunch?

Frank-footers.

Where did Cyclops go on his vacation?

An eye-land cruise.

Why did Cyclops have to close his school?

He had only one pupil.

What's one thing Cyclops always overlooks?

His nose.

Why was Cyclops jealous of the Mississippi River?

It has four eyes (i's).

Why does Cyclops like China and Haiti?

Because they both have an i (eye)
in the middle.

**What was Cyclops's favorite thing
to see in Paris?**

The Eye-ful Tower.

**Can Bigfoot jump higher than
a 20-foot wall?**

Yes, because a 20-foot wall can't jump.

**Why did people think the Headless
Horseman was crazy?**

His mind was gone.

What did one zombie say to the other zombie?

"Get a life!"

What did King Kong say after falling off the Empire State Building?

"One more time from the top."

How did the Blob cross the road?

In a goo kart.

Why did the Blob cross the road?

To goo to the other side.

**What should you say when
the Blob tells a joke?**

"Yuck-yuck."

**What do you call it when the Blob
visits Munchkinland?**

Ooze and Oz.

Where are most horror movies made?

Howl-ywood.

Who is the scariest writer?

R. L. Franken-Stine.

Why did the Blob eat the lamp store?

It wanted to be brighter.

What man has three eyes and can't be seen?

The Invisible Man (three i's).

What did the monster say to the Invisible Man?

"I can see right through you."

How do you say "Cyclops" in German?

"Cyclops in German."

Godzilla: The doctor told me to drink some lemon juice after a hot bath.

King Kong: Did you drink the lemon juice?

Godzilla: No, I haven't finished drinking the hot bath yet.

What do you get if you cross King Kong and a kangaroo?

A huge fur coat with one pocket in it.

What do you get if you cross Godzilla with a rooster?

A monster that can wake people who live in top-floor apartments.

What did the Headless Horseman say to his horse when it was time to eat?

"Hay there."

Why was it easy to understand everything the Invisible Man said?

He was perfectly clear.

What is the Blob's favorite beverage?

Slime-ade.

What's big, hairy, and bounces?

Bigfoot on a trampoline.

10

ONE-LINERS

"Nobody can see me," the Invisible Man said clearly.

"I'm feeling full of energy today," the electric eel said glowingly.

"Yikes! There are no bones at the end of my arm!" the skeleton said offhandedly.

"Gimme a hug," the porcupine said sharply.

"Like to buy a coffin?" the undertaker said gravely.

"Come closer," the poison-ivy monster said rashly.

"That ghost movie was terrible!" Tom booed.

"The funeral car has a flat and
there's no spare in the trunk,"
the driver said tirelessly.

Every time the sea monster sneezed,
it started a tidal wave.

Remember to say "thank you" when
sucking someone's blood.

People are dying to get into
that graveyard.

The Abominable Snowman rode
an icicle to work.

Ask someone, "If cold tea is iced tea, what is cold ink?" When they say "iced ink," it sounds like "I stink." Gotcha!

Ask someone, "If old tea is used tea, what is old ink?" When they say "used ink," it sounds like "You stink." You got yourself!

Have someone say this magic phrase, "O wah ta foo lie am," and it will sound like they're saying, "Oh, what a fool I am."

Did you hear about the ghost that was so small it couldn't fill a sheet and had to use a pillowcase instead?

After eating Tokyo, Godzilla was
hungry again an hour later.

If you rearrange the letters in
"Frankenstein," it spells "ten freaks inn."

Do skeletons eat elbow macaroni?

The story of how Frankenstein's
monster came to life is shocking.

Hamburger:
The sound a werewolf makes in
Hamburg, Germany (Hamburg, grr).

The monster spent hundreds of dollars on deodorants before discovering that people didn't like him anyway.

The evil magician liked to saw people in half...which is why he had half-brothers and half-sisters.

Wizard: Doctor, every time I say "abracadabra," a person disappears... Doctor? Doctor, are you there?

The short fortune-teller who escaped from prison was a small medium at large.

Did you hear about the sick toad? It croaked.

The old ogre had teeth like stars—
they came out at night.

I wish I had a genie. (Think about it.)

How do you do voodoo?

Frankenstein's attorney was
a monster-in-law.

That witch uses a crystal ball,
but I don't know what she sees in it.

Put an **OGRE** in a blender, mix it up
good, and you get **GORE**.

The big dance for...

...Bigfoot was the foot ball.

...Cyclops was the eye ball.

...the Abominable Snowman was the snow ball.

...the Blob was the slime ball.

...Frankenstein's monster was the screw ball.

...Wolfman was the hair ball.

...the skeleton was the stick ball.

...the sea monster was the beach ball.

...the ogre was the foul ball.

...the scarecrow was the corn ball.

...the T. rex was the t-ball.

...the grave digger was the dirt ball.

...the bat was the air ball.

...the skunk was the stink ball.

...the gummy bear was the gum ball.

...the octopus was the eight ball.

...the dragon was the fire ball.

...the witch was the black ball.

...the three-legged ghoul was the odd ball.

...the chicken was the fowl ball.

...the wizard was the crystal ball.

The grave digger's coffee tasted like mud because it was just ground that morning.

Rearranging all the letters in DR. FRANKENSTEIN'S MONSTER will spell MR. FIEND'S ROTTEN RANKNESS.

Run away if a vampire asks to stop over for a bite.

Did you hear about the ghoul's
new daytime talk show?
It's called *Phantom of the Oprah*.

Dracula puts the "vein" in Transylvania.

Don't worry about the goblin that
lost her left leg and left arm.
She's all right now.

The girl put a sheet over her head
for Halloween...and went as
an unmade bed.

Knock-knock!
Who's there?
Dracula.
Dracula who?
Dracula doesn't have a last name, silly!

How do gourds get stronger?

By pumpkin iron.

11

GHOULISH GAGS

Why are goblins covered in wrinkles?

Have you ever tried ironing one?

Ogre: I thought an onion was the only food that would make me cry... until a frightened little girl threw a coconut in my face.

Ogre 1: Do you think I'm pretty or ugly?

Ogre 2: You're both.

Ogre 1: What do you mean?

Ogre 2: You're pretty ugly.

What are green and fly around beaches?

Seaghouls.

Old goblin: Someone told me I have the body of a 20-year-old goblin.

Old ogre: Well, give it back, you're getting it all wrinkled!

Ogre 1: Which do you like better, my good looks or my good smile?

Ogre 2: Your good sense of humor.

How did the ghoul lose weight?

He started going to
Ogre-eaters Anonymous.

Ogre 1: Do these pants make me look fat?

Ogre 2: No, what's inside them does.

Why did the chicken cross the road?

To get to the ugly ogre's house.

Knock-knock!

Who's there?

The chicken.

Teacher: I asked you to draw a ghoul and a goblin, and you drew only a ghoul. Where's the goblin?

Student: The ghoul ate it.

What do you call a hobgoblin that collects coins?

A hobby-goblin.

How can you tell when a hobgoblin is dizzy?

When he's hobwobblin' down the street.

What do you call a hobgoblin that's...

...crying? A sobgoblin.

...messy? A slobgoblin.

...eating corn? A cobgoblin.

...employed? A jobgoblin.

...stuck up? A snobgoblin.

...in a gang? A mobgoblin.

...taken your wallet? A robgoblin.

...been turned into a doodad?
A thingamobgoblin.

What do ogres call slow-moving people?

Dinner.

**What do you call
an average-looking ogre?**

A mediogre.

What do you call an overweight ogre?

A meaty ogre.

Why was Shrek late?

He ogre slept (overslept).

What's a gnome's favorite city?

Gnome, Alaska.

**What do you call it when you
have to choose between a gnome
and not a gnome?**

Gnome or Mr. Nice Guy
(no more Mr. Nice Guy).

What two letters did the 50-foot-tall
woman say when she met
a 25-foot-tall monster?

I W.

What did the giant cough up after
eating a werewolf?

A hair ball.

A giant named Mrs. Bigger had
a baby. Which was bigger,
the baby or Mrs. Bigger?

The baby, because it was a little Bigger.

What smells and goes
thump, squish, thump, squish?

A giant who's stepped in dragon poop.

If storks bring human babies,
what bring giant babies?

Cranes.

What do you get if you cross
a pen with a giant?

The Ink-credible Hulk.

How does the 50-foot-tall woman
put on lipstick?

With a paint roller.

Knock-knock!

Who's there.

Sarah.

Sarah who?

Sarah giant living in there?

What says, "Muf, of, if, eef"?

A giant walking backward.

Why didn't the giant have any teeth?

Because he slept with his head
under his pillow and the fairies
kept taking them.

What did the chewing gum
say to the giant?

"I'm stuck on you."

What is a giant's favorite game?

Swallow the leader.

How do you talk to a giant?

Use big words.

Why did the giant get a headache
every time he was thirsty?

Because he would walk into
a bar to get a drink.

**Why did the giant have big holes
in his underwear?**

To get his legs through.

Why do ducks have wide, webbed feet?

To stamp out fires.

Why do giants have big, flat feet?

To stamp out burning ducks.

**What do you get if you cross
a giraffe and an ant?**

A giant.

What's higher up than a giant?

A giant's hat.

Why do giants like gnomes?

Their cone hats make them easier to eat.

What kind of college did the Swamp Thing go to?

Ivy League.

Why do sea monsters live in salt water?

Because pepper water makes them sneeze.

Why did the sea monster do poorly in school?

Because it was under C (undersea) level.

Why did the sea monster blush?

It saw the ocean's bottom.

What did the sea monster say when it was confused?

"Could you be more Pacific, please?"

Why was the sea monster yellow and smelly?

Because the sea weed.

12

HALLOWEEN HUMOR

Why were the candy man's feet sore?

He had candy corns on them.

What do you get if you cross a candy corn and a werewolf?

A corn dog.

What do you call stolen Hershey bars on Halloween?

Hot chocolate.

What do you call a cow that can't moo?

A milk dud.

What do you get if you put candy in a plate of spaghetti?

Sweetish meatballs.

What candy bar likes Halloween jokes?

Snickers.

What did Mr. Goodbar give
Almond Joy?

Chocolate kisses.

Why did the Oreo cookie go
to the dentist?

It lost its filling.

What is a monkey's favorite kind
of cookie?

Chocolate chimp.

What is a mummy's favorite candy?

M&MMy's.

What kind of candy bar is for girls only?

A her-she bar.

What Halloween candy smells the worst?

Footsie Rolls.

What does a 3 Musketeers bar hear with?

Six musket-ears.

Why don't they give prisoners chocolate on Halloween?

Because they break out.

What candy bar does a dog like to eat?

Kit Kat.

What's the happiest candy bar?

Almond Joy.

Why did the man spill coffee all over the kitchen counter?

He tried to pour it into a Reese's Peanut Butter Cup.

Why don't skeletons go trick-or-treating on cold nights?

The wind goes right through them.

**Why did the Halloween cookie
go to the hospital?**

It was feeling crumby.

What's a good kind of scarecrow?

One that's outstanding in its field.

**What did the alien cat say when
it landed on Earth?**

"Take me to your litter."

How does an alien count to 10?

On its eyeballs.

What kind of alien has 36 toes?

One with three feet.

How do aliens make a trip around the solar system?

They planet (plan it).

Why do aliens prefer eating asteroids more than comets?

They're meteor.

How do you keep an alien baby from crying?

You rocket (rock it).

Knock-knock!
Who's there?
Europe.
Europe who?
No, you're a poo!

Knock-knock!
Who's there?
Who who.
Who who who?
What are you laughing at?

Knock-knock!
Who's there?
What, where, when, why.
What, where, when, why who?
What are you, a reporter?

Knock-knock!

Who's there?

Chalk.

Chalk who?

**Chocolate is my favorite
on Halloween.**

Knock-knock!

Who's there?

Handsome.

Handsome who?

Handsome candy to me.

Knock-knock!

Who's there?

Wanda.

Wanda who?

Wanda go trick-or-treating with me?

Knock-knock!
Who's there?
Hans.
Hans who?
Hans off the candy.

Knock-knock!
Who's there?
I'm Gladys.
I'm Gladys who?
I'm Gladys Halloween.

Knock-knock!
Who's there?
Hugo.
Hugo who?
Hugo put on a costume.

Knock-knock!

Who's there?

Al.

Al who?

Al trade you a Snickers for a Kit Kat.

Knock-knock!

Who's there?

Butter.

Butter who?

Butter fill up my bag with candy.

Knock-knock!

Who's there?

Omar.

Omar who?

Omar gosh, that's a scary costume!

Knock-knock!
Who's there?
Art.
Art who?
R2-D2, of course!

Knock-knock!
Who's there?
Stopwatch.
Stopwatch who?
**Stopwatch you're doing and
open this door.**

Knock-knock!
Who's there?
Costume.
Costume who?
**Costume much to buy a costume,
so I'm going as myself.**

Knock-knock!

Who's there?

Sour.

Sour who?

Sour you doing?

Knock-knock!

Who's there?

Wooden leg.

Wooden leg who?

Wooden leg go of that candy
if I were you!

Knock-knock!

Who's there?

Doolittle.

Doolittle who?

Doolittle monsters grow up
to be big monsters?

13

GOURD GIGGLES

Why did the girl carve George Washington's face into her pumpkin?

She wanted to be a George Washington Carver.

What's orange and can't climb trees?

A pumpkin.

GOURD GIGGLES

What has warts, can cast spells,
and flies through the sky?

A magical gourd.

What's the worst thing about
pumpkin pie?

When it's all eaten.

What's the very first thing that comes
out of a pumpkin when carving it?

The #1 seed.

What did the pumpkin say
to the celery?

"Stop stalking me!"

Why do people like corn mazes?

Because pumpkin mazes are too easy.

**You throw away my insides,
cut up my outside, and eat neither.
What food am I?**

A pumpkin.

**What can you find on a pumpkin's
inside and outside in the morning?**

Pumpkin seed, pumpkin dew.

**Why didn't the pumpkin tell
jokes to the eggs?**

It didn't want to crack them up.

What did the pumpkin vine say to the little pumpkin?

"You're starting to grow on me."

What's a pumpkin's favorite horror movie?

Silence of the Yams.

What do you call the bottom of a pumpkin?

The rumpkin.

What goes *sproing, splat*?

A jumping pumpkin.

If you have two pumpkins in one hand and three in the other, what do you have?

Really big hands!

When is a pumpkin not a pumpkin?

When it's pumpkin else.

What do pumpkins and noses have in common?

They're both picked.

What do pumpkins and mink pups have in common?

They're both spelled with the same letters.

Why were the pumpkins secretive?

Because the potatoes had eyes
and the corn had ears.

**What crop did the farmer plant
next to the pumpkins?**

Beets me!

Where are little pumpkins sent to grow?

Kinder-garden.

How do you make a pumpkin turnover?

Roll it down a hill.

Why do people bob for apples on Halloween?

Because pumpkins are too big.

What is the left side of a pumpkin pie?

The side you haven't eaten yet.

What can a whole pumpkin do that half a pumpkin can't?

Look round.

First jack-o'-lantern: You look sad. What's eating you?

Second jack-o'-lantern: Squirrels, I think.

GOURD GIGGLES

Why was the pumpkin unhappy?

Teams were formed, and it wasn't picked.

Why wouldn't the gourd speak to the pumpkin pie?

It was too flaky.

What did the pumpkin say after Halloween?

"Good-pie, everyone."

Why did the pumpkin pie crust go to the dentist?

It needed a filling.

**What do you get if you cross a train
with a pumpkin pie?**

Puff pastry.

**What did the pumpkin pie say
to the pecan pie?**

"You're nuts!"

**If it took one kid 20 minutes to eat
a pumpkin pie, how long would
it take two kids to eat it?**

They can't eat it.
The other kid already did.

Why did the pumpkin pie cross the road?

It saw a fork up ahead.

GOURD GIGGLES

Why did the vegetable farmer refuse to grow pumpkins?

Because pumpkins are fruit.
(No, that's not funny—but it's true!)

Why did the man eat a pumpkin pie in his race car?

He liked fast food.

Person 1: I just burned 2,000 calories in 20 minutes.

Person 2: How?

Person 1: I forgot to take my pumpkin pie out of the oven.

Try saying this pumpkin pie tongue twister three times fast:

"Some cinnamon is in 'em."

Why did the candle keep going out inside the pumpkin?

Because the pumpkin was a light eater.

Why do jack-o'-lanterns have stupid smiles on their faces?

You would too if you'd just had all your brains scooped out.

Why were the two pumpkins so close?

They had deep roots.

What do you call a pumpkin's hat?

Stem wear (stemware).

Why was the jack-o'-lantern jealous of the glass of orange juice?

It still had lots of pulp in it.

How can you tell when a jack-o'-lantern is glad to see you?

Its face lights up.

Why did the jack-o'-lantern turn away from the radio?

It couldn't face the music.

What do you call it when you pick up a jack-o'-lantern?

A face-lift.

How do you turn on an electric jack-o'-lantern?

By plugging in the electric gourd.

What's the difference between a pumpkin and a rock?

Rock pie doesn't taste nearly as good.

Who do jack-o'-lanterns date?

Jill-o'-lanterns.

14

MUMMIES AND MORE

What happened when Dracula bit
the Abominable Snowman?

He became cold blooded.

How did Dracula look after
he got glasses?

Spec-tacula!

What is Dracula's favorite board game?

Bat-tleship.

How do you say goodbye to a room full of vampires?

"So long, suckers!"

What did the cackling witch and Dracula name their baby?

Cackula.

Why couldn't the mummy go to the party?

It was tied up.

Do mummies give live interviews?

No, they're always taped.

What is a mummy's favorite kind of music?

Ragtime.

Why was the Egyptian king sad?

He lost his mummy.

What kind of climate does a mummy like best?

Embalmy weather.

What kind of roads are mummies born on?

Winding roads.

What does a mummy write at the top of a letter?

"Tomb it may concern."

What two things do you call a mummified king with children?

Mummy *and* daddy.

Who are the most famous mummies?

Rap stars (wrap stars).

What did the mummy maker say when she finished making the mummy?

"OK, that's a wrap!"

What did the mummy mommy say to her mummy son?

"Tut-tut, Tut."

Why didn't the mummy go to the party?

He was too wrapped up in his work.

Where do mummies go for pizza?

Pizza Tut.

**What is a zombie's favorite
winter sport?**

Disfigure skating.

**What part of a zombie smells
the most?**

His nose.

**What is a zombie's favorite
summer sport?**

The die-cathlon.

Why didn't the zombie go to school?

He felt rotten.

Why didn't the zombie go to school?

She was dead tired.

Why don't zombie children behave?

They're spoiled.

What kind of candy will a zombie never eat?

Life Savers.

Knock-knock!
Who's there?
Weed.
Weed who?
Weed better get away from these zombies!

What country do zombies come from?

The contami-nation.

What do you call buzzing insects that come back to life?

Zom-bees.

When do zombies succeed?

When they're dead ahead.

Why does Dracula get out of his coffin to solve problems?

He likes to think outside the box.

What's the difference between someone who writes music and a zombie?

One composes, the other decomposes.

What magazine did the zombie look at after eating everyone in the library?

Reader's Digest.

Where do zombies eat at home?

The living dead room.

What is a zombie's favorite bean to eat?

A human bean.

What do you call a zombie telemarketer?

A dead ringer.

What was the zombie given when he showed up late for dinner?

The cold shoulder.

What streets do zombies live on?

Dead-end streets.

What did Mr. Wonderful say to the zombie on *Shark Tank*?

"You're dead to me."

What is a zombie's favorite shampoo?

Head & Shoulders.

Why did the zombie lose his lawsuit?

He didn't have a leg to stand on.

Why did the zombie stop eating the comedian?

He tasted funny.

Why was the zombie expelled from school?

She kept buttering up her teacher.

What does a zombie use to get around?

A blood vessel.

What should you get if you have
a zombie living next door?

Life insurance.

What did the zombies eat at
the barbecue?

Handburgers.

What's the best way to find a zombie?

Buried.

**What do you call zombies
who eat and run?**

Zoom-bies.

**When does a zombie need to
spell things out?**

When he's competing in a zom-bee.

**What room in the house is least likely
to have a zombie in it?**

The living room.

Who did the zombie invite to the party?

Anyone he could dig up.

15

SPOOKY STUFF

What is a ghost's motto?

"Eat, drink, and be scary."

What did the skeleton order
with his drink?

A mop.

**What did the monsters call
the bumbling skeleton?**

Bonehead.

Why was the skeleton afraid?

He was gutless.

**What do you say when a skeleton
is leaving on a trip?**

"Bone voyage!"

What is a skeleton most afraid of?

A pack of hungry dogs.

What Halloween creatures weigh the most?

Skele-tons.

What did the skeleton couple open at the bank?

A joint account.

What do skeletons keep in a first-aid kit?

Spare ribs.

How do you make a skeleton laugh?

Tickle his funny bone.

What is a skeleton's least favorite type of dancing?

Break dancing.

Why can't skeletons play church music?

They have no organs.

Why did the skeleton cross the road?

To go to the body shop.

Where do skeletons go before college?

High skull.

What musical instrument is a skeleton's favorite?

The trom-bone.

What is a skeleton's favorite horse?

A night mare.

Why don't skeletons like to ride horses?

They prefer riding bonies.

Where did the skeletons go for food and drinks?

A hip joint.

Why didn't the skeleton like Halloween candy?

He didn't have the stomach for it.

Why didn't the skeleton dance at the Halloween party?

He had no body to dance with.

Why are skeletons mean?

Because they're heartless.

What kind of questions are skeletons best at answering?

No-brainers.

Who was the most famous French skeleton?

Napoleon Bone-apart.

What do you call a skeleton wearing a T-shirt?

T-bones.

What do you call a skeleton that sleeps late?

Lazy bones.

Why are skeletons always so relaxed?

Because nothing gets under their skin.

What do you call a hopeful skeleton?

Wishbones.

Why did the skeleton put ground beef on his knee?

So it would be a burger joint.

What was the skeleton after staying out in the cold all night?

A numbskull.

What type of art do skeletons like best?

Skull-pture.

What do you call snake skeletons?

Rattlers.

What happened to the skeleton who sat by the fire all day?

He became bone dry.

What kind of plates do skeletons eat off of?

Bone china.

What's a skeleton's favorite song?

"Bone to Be Wild."

How did the grave digger organize
his family reunion?

He dug up some old relatives.

What's a good name for an undertaker?

Barry (bury).

Why is a cemetery a great place
to write a story?

Because there are so many plots in it.

Where are cemeteries usually located?

In the dead center of town.

Woman: That cemetery is huge. I wonder how many dead people are in it.

Man: All of them.

What happened when the computer was left in the haunted forest?

The trees logged on.

What was the grave digger's favorite clue in the crossword puzzle?

6 Down.

What's the best way to find a haunted house?

Empty.

What was left after they cut down the haunted forest?

Haunted sawdust.

Why were the trees in the haunted forest scared?

They were petrified.

What kind of key opens a haunted house?

A spoo-key.

Who keeps ghosts safe at the beach?

The ghost guard.

What kind of waterways sound like the floors in a haunted house?

Creeks.

Knock-knock!
Who's there?
Dishes.
Dishes who?
Dishes a very scary house.

Knock-knock!
Who's there?
Boo.
Boo who?
Are you a ghost or an owl?
Make up your mind.

16

FRANKENSTEIN AND FRIENDS

Try saying this three times quickly:

"Mister Monster mastered mysteries."

Why was the monster recruited for the basketball team?

Because he was good at dribbling.

Ghoul: I can lift a monster with one hand.

Goblin: Bet you can't!

Ghoul: Find me a monster with one hand, and I'll prove it!

Did you hear about the monster with five legs?

His pants fit him like a glove.

What did the monster say when he visited a classroom full of kids?

"Pleased to eat you."

How did the monster lose 20 pounds of ugly fat?

He cut off his head.

What do young female monsters do at parties?

They look for edible bachelors.

How do monsters count to 100?

On their warts.

What do you call a huge, slobbering monster with fluffy hair growing out of his ears?

Anything you want, he can't hear you.

Monster 1: I'm so thirsty my tongue is hanging out.

Monster 2: Oh, I thought that was your tie.

What did the monster mom tell her children at the dinner table?

"It's not polite to talk with someone in your mouth."

What's the best kind of fur to get from a monster?

As fur away as possible.

What do you get if you cross a plum with a man-eating monster?

A purple people eater.

What did the monsters have to eat at the all-you-can-eat buffet?

The waiters.

How do you greet
a three-headed monster?

"Hi. How are you? What's new?"

How do monsters like their eggs?

Terror-fried.

What was the monster's favorite
place to swim?

Lake Eerie.

What two places did the mad scientist
like to go to on vacation?

Mad-rid and Mad-agascar.

**What kind of dog did
the mad scientist have?**

A Lab.

**Who did Frankenstein's monster
bring to the dance?**

His ghoulfriend.

**What time was it when the townspeople
chased Frankenstein's monster?**

Twenty after one.

**What did Dr. Frankenstein say to his
monster just before bringing it to life?**

"Lie down, you're in for a shock."

What news did Frankenstein's
monster like best?

Current events.

Can you avoid getting hurt by
Frankenstein's monster if
you run away from it?

Depends on how fast you run.

How many bolts were used to create
Frankenstein's monster?

Three. Two bolts for the neck and a
lightning bolt from the sky.

Why did Frankenstein's monster take a whole bottle of aspirin?

He had a monstrous headache.

Why did Frankenstein's monster roam the countryside looking for other monsters?

He was playing Pokémon Go.

Why did Dr. Frankenstein hire Igor as his assistant?

He had a hunch about him.

What does the bride of Frankenstein put in her hair?

Scare spray.

Dr. Frankenstein: Igor, stand over here by the window and stick your tongue out.

Igor: Why, doctor? Do you think I'm coming down with something?

Dr. Frankenstein: No, I'm mad at those noisy villagers outside.

Dr. Frankenstein: My monster should live to be 80.

Igor: The brain you put in him was 80 years old.

Dr. Frankenstein: See, I was right!

What goes *stomp, stomp, thump*?

Frankenstein's monster losing his head during a temper tantrum.

What did Frankenstein's monster call a screwdriver?

Daddy.

What has a head with two bolts in it and says *oink*?

Franken-swine.

How do you keep Dr. Frankenstein from charging?

Take away his credit card.

What does it say on the tomb of Frankenstein's monster?

Rest in pieces.

**Why did Frankenstein's monster
never have any money?**

Because he was charged a lot
when staying at the castle.

**What would you call Dr. Frankenstein
if he had an extra eye?**

Dr. Frankensteini.

**What goes
clomp, clomp, sproing, sproing?**

Frankenstein's monster doing
the bunny hop.

How did Dr. Frankenstein
get around town?

He drove a monster truck.

What is Dr. Frankenstein's favorite
baseball team?

The New York Frankees.

Why did Dr. Frankenstein flunk
out of wizard school?

He couldn't spell.

Why couldn't Frankenstein's
monster stop laughing?

Because Dr. Frankenstein
had him in stitches.

What did one of Frankenstein's monster's ears say to the other?

I didn't know we lived on the same block.

How did Dr. Frankenstein get his monster's mind working?

He waited for a brainstorm.

Why did Dr. Frankenstein take his monster's nose apart?

To see what made it run.

17

What do you call a witch in a T-shirt?

Twitch.

What's under a witch's teacup when she's on her broom?

A flying saucer.

What do witches wear on their wrists?

Charm bracelets.

**Why do witches wear pointy,
black hats?**

To keep their heads warm.

Why did the witch feed her cat pennies?

She wanted to put money in the kitty.

**What do you call witches
when they're in bed?**

Sleeping bags.

Why was the witch's broom late?

It overswept.

Why did the witch use a computer to write new magical chants?

Because it had spell check.

What do you call it when a witch forgets a spell?

Hex-agon.

What did the prince say after the witch turned him into a frog?

"Ribbit!"

What does a witch write with?

Magic Markers.

**What does an evil magician like
to keep up his sleeve?**

His arm.

**What do you call a wizard
on an airplane?**

A flying sorcerer.

**What do you get if you cross
a wizard and a blizzard?**

A cold spell.

Why was the magician flat and hard?

He was driving his car and turned
in to a driveway.

**What did the woman say after
the magician sawed her in half?**

"Thanks for halving me."

What was on the magician's test?

Trick questions.

**What does a sick magician
keep up his sleeves?**

Get-well cards.

Why did the wizard wear a yellow
cape to the Halloween party?

He was going as a banana.

What's one thing each year that
a fire-breathing dragon can't do?

Blow out the candles on
its birthday cake.

What do you call a princess when
she steps on a banana peel?

Slipping Beauty.

What do you get if you cross
a big black dog and a magician?

A labracadabrador.

What do you call fairies that don't take baths?

Fairy (very) smelly.

What do elves learn in school?

The elf-abet.

What happened when the wizard misbehaved at school?

He was ex-spelled.

How does a wizard make a rock float?

Root beer, one scoop of ice cream, and a rock.

**Who's the most famous
wizard detective?**

Warlock Holmes.

What do you call a wizard who's lost?

A wand-erer.

What did the dragon say to the knight?

"Drat, canned food again."

**Why do dragons always
know their weight?**

Because they have lots of scales.

Why are dragons boring?

Because they have long tails.

What award did the dragon win in the beauty contest?

Beast in show.

Why do dragons sleep during the day?

So they can fight knights.

What did Cinderella say when her photos weren't delivered?

Someday my prints will come.

**Why did the young wizard go
to bed every night?**

Because he couldn't get
the bed to come to him.

**What's worse than
a fire-breathing dragon?**

A fire-breathing dragon that sneezes.

**If you're an intruder, and the castle
is locked, how do you get in?**

Intruder window
(in through the window).

When is a castle door not a door?

When it's ajar.

What runs around a castle but never moves?

A moat.

Dragon 1: It feels kind of hot in here.

Dragon 2: Stop breathing so hard!

What do you call a rich elf?

Welfy.

What's the last thing you see when a fairy is flying away from you?

A fairy tail.

**What has wings and gives you
an offer you can't refuse?**

The Fairy Godfather.

**What does the tooth fairy
use to fix her wand?**

Tooth paste.

What do you call a witch with one leg?

Eileen (I lean).

**Why did the witch wear ugly
yellow stockings?**

Because her ugly purple ones
were at the cleaners.

18

KOOKY CREATURES

What do you call a mad cow on the dance floor?

Beef jerky.

What's sweet and puts out fires?

Gummy the Bear.

KOOKY CREATURES

Where can you find dead snakes?

Right where you left them.

**What do you call two spiders
that just got married?**

Newlywebbed.

**Where can you find bats, then cats,
and, a little while later, rats?**

In the dictionary.

Knock-knock!
Who's there?
Gorilla.
Gorilla who?
Gorilla me a cheese sandwich please.

KOOKY CREATURES

What do cats like to sing?

Mews-ic.

How many tickles does it take to make an octopus laugh?

Ten tickles.

What did the slug say when it crawled on the turtle's back?

"Wheeeeee!"

What do you call a sheep with no legs?

A cloud.

What do you call grizzly bears with no ears?

Grizzly b.

What kind of bird has wings but can't fly?

A dead bird.

Why are frogs always so happy?

They eat whatever bugs them.

What do you call an alligator wearing a vest?

An investi-gator.

KOOKY CREATURES

What has more lives than a cat?

A frog, because it croaks every night.

Why did the centipede lie on its side?

It wanted to be 100 feet tall.

Why can't you hear a pterodactyl go to the bathroom?

Because the *p* (pee) is silent.

What do you call a dinosaur with a big vocabulary?

A thesaurus.

What are invisible and smell like mice?

Cat farts.

Baby snake: Mommy, are we poisonous?

Mommy snake: Yes, why do you ask?

Baby snake: Because I just bit myself.

What do you call a man who's been attacked by a cat?

Claude.

Where do baby apes sleep?

In apri-cots.

What's the difference between a bird and a fly?

A bird can fly but a fly can't bird.

Why do gorillas have such big nostrils?

Because they have such big fingers.

What is a snake's favorite dance?

The mamba.

What kind of bird do snakes like best?

Swallows.

KOOKY CREATURES

**How can you tell if a snake
is really upset?**

It throws a hissy fit.

What kind of snake likes pumpkin pie?

A pumpkin pie-thon.

**What do you call a snake that
builds things?**

A boa constructor.

Who takes care of a king cobra?

His serpents.

KOOKY CREATURES

What do you get when you cross a snake with a kangaroo?

A jump rope.

What do you give a sick snake?

Asp-irin.

What is a snake's favorite vegetable?

Coily-flower (cauliflower).

What do friendly cobras have?

Good poisonalities.

What subject are snakes good
at in school?

Hiss-tory.

Why are most snakes safe to go near?

Because they're unarmed.

Why did the two boa constrictors
get married?

They had a crush on each other.

What should you do if you find a snake
sleeping in your bed?

Sleep on the sofa.

What treat do snakes like to get on Halloween?

Wrigley's gum.

Which hand should you use to pick up a dangerous snake?

Someone else's.

What do you get if you cross a pig and a snake?

A boar constrictor.

What Hogwarts house do snakes belong to?

Slitherin' (Slytherin).

KOOKY CREATURES

**What do you do if you find
a cobra in your toilet?**

Wait until it's finished.

**What do you get if you cross
a snake with a hot dog?**

A fang-furter.

**Why did the snake have
trouble speaking?**

It had a frog in its throat.

Why are snakes hard to fool?

You can't pull their leg.

KOOKY CREATURES

What did the snake put on its floor?

Rep-tiles.

**Why did the chameleon jump
in the blender?**

To blend in.

What was the iguana's favorite movie?

The Lizard of Oz.

**What do you call a werewolf that knows
everything that's going on?**

An aware-wolf.

19

BEASTLY BEINGS

What do you call a pan after King Kong steps on it?

A pancake.

What do you call it when King Kong dials the wrong telephone number?

Ring wrong.

What would you need if you crossed King Kong and a dog?

A huge pooper-scooper.

How do you catch King Kong?

Hang upside down and make a noise like a banana.

What do you get if King Kong steps on your feet?

Flat feet.

What did the checkout clerk say to the Abominable Snowman?

"Have an ice day."

What do you get if you cross the Abominable Snowman and Dracula?

Frostbite.

What business is King Kong in?

Monkey business.

What's King Kong's brother's name?

Hong Kong.

Who did King Kong marry?

Queen Kong.

What is as big as King Kong but doesn't weigh anything?

King Kong's shadow.

If King Kong ate a Ding Dong while playing Ping-Pong and died, what would they put on his coffin?

A lid.

If King Kong twists his ankle, how can it be fixed?

With a monkey wrench.

Why did King Kong climb the Empire State Building?

Because he wouldn't fit in the elevator.

What did Godzilla's mom say when Godzilla attacked ships in the harbor?

"Quit playing with your toys and finish your bath!"

Why didn't Godzilla eat the hotel?

He was trying to cut down on suites.

What's the biggest problem for the Loch Ness Monster?

Lonely Ness.

What did they call the Abominable Snowman after doing 100 sit-ups?

The Abdominal Snowman.

What was the Abominable Snowman before he was the Abominable Snowman?

The Abominable Snowboy.

What does the Abominable Snowman take when he gets hot?

A chill pill.

What's the Abominable Snowman's favorite cereal?

Ice Krispies.

What's the Abominable Snowman's second-favorite cereal?

Frosted Flakes.

Who visits the Abominable Snowman on Father's Day?

His chill-dren.

Why were the Abominable Snowman's feet yellow?

Ask the Abominable Snowdog.

How does the Abominable Snowman get to work?

In his Abominable Snowmobile.

Why was the Abominable Snowman yawning?

He was snow bored (snowboard).

How do Abominable Snowmen greet each other?

With cold waves.

How does the Abominable Snowman get his hair dry?

He freeze-dries it.

What do you call a Bigfoot that works with clay?

Hairy potter.

What do they call Bigfoot in Canada?

Big Thirty Centimeters.

What do you call a ditzy Abominable Snowman?

A snowflake.

What did the Abominable Snowman say when he got back from vacation?

"There's snow place like home."

Where does the Abominable Snowman keep his money?

In a snowbank.

What is the Abominable Snowman's favorite food?

Chili (chilly).

What is the Abominable Snowman's favorite song?

"Freeze a Jolly Good Fellow."

What do you call the Abominable Snowman in Florida?

A puddle.

What do you call the Abominable Snowman in Pittsburgh?

Lost.

Why did the Abominable Snowman skip going to the party?

He got cold feet.

What does the Hunchback of Notre Dame do every morning?

Gargoyle with mouthwash.

What are bigger than King Kong's feet?

King Kong's shoes.

What fruit does King Kong like best?

Ape-ricots.

Why did King Kong join the army?

He wanted to learn gorilla warfare.

Would you rather have King Kong chase you or Godzilla?

I'd rather have King Kong chase Godzilla.

Why couldn't Godzilla disguise himself?

Because disguise the limit.

What does the Invisible Man write letters with?

Invisible ink.

What's the worst job in Transylvania?

Being a dogcatcher on nights when the moon is full.

**What do you call a horror movie
that does really poorly?**

A bomb scare.

**What did the artists use to draw
the *Monsters, Inc.* characters?**

Monsters ink.

**How can you communicate with
the Loch Ness Monster?**

Drop it a line.

20

WORDPLAY AND WISECRACKS

Teacher: Can you use "cattle" in a sentence about Halloween?

Girl: I can't—but I bet that black cat'll (cattle) do it.

What do you get if you cross...

...a ghost and a monster? A booster.

...a pig and a monster? A hamster.

...a kangaroo and a monster?
A rooster.

...an angry crowd and a monster?
A mobster.

...a tennis player and a monster?
A lobster.

**If women get their hair done at
beauty parlors, do witches get their
hair done at ugly parlors?**

**The phrase "living legend" gets
a lot creepier if you add a space to
the last word: "living leg end."**

Dr. Awkward spelled backward is...
Dr. Awkward!

When Dr. Frankenstein ordered a hot
dog and a mug of root beer for lunch...
he got a frank and stein.

Bacteria:
the rear entrance to a cafeteria.

Witchcraft: another name for a broom.

Death sentence:
a one-liner graveyard joke.

Deadlines: stuff written on gravestones.

Cheerios: Hula-Hoops for Ant-Man.

Nothing: a boneless skeleton.

What apartment did these monsters live in...

...Cyclops: 1-I.

...the cannibal: 8-U.

...the old witch: 9-T.

...Wolfman: K-9.

...the ill pirate: C-6.

...a zombie's victim: E-10.

Harvest:
what a joke-telling scarecrow wears.

Alienation:
a country where space creatures live.

Vamoose:
a vampire with large antlers.

The Headless Horseman was
hot to trot after running into
the fire-breathing dragon.

Did you hear the joke about the ghost's
broken drum? It can't be beat.

It was very humid and the werewolf
was having a bad hair day.

Snake charmers use vipers to
clean off their vindshields.

The problem with witch twins is that
you never know which witch is which.

Is a mummy that snacks in bed
a crumby mummy?

Is a smelly monster's little finger
a stinky pinky?

Is a mummy with no teeth
a gummy mummy?

Is a witch who touches poison ivy
an itchy witchy?

If Dracula buys bacon,
is he a ham-buyer vampire?

Is a slobbery goblin a drool ghoul?

Is a ghoul with a sprained ankle
a hobblin' goblin?

Is a female snake a hiss miss?

Did you hear about the vampire
magazine? It was nothing but bat news.

A mummy will listen to you
in rapt attention.

That dragon had such a big mouth it
could eat a banana sideways.

Did you hear the joke about
the fungus? It grows on you.

Riddle: The maker doesn't keep it,
the buyer doesn't use it, and
the user doesn't see it. What is it?
Answer: A coffin.

Dracula wrote a formula about
a tarantula on the peninsula.

Never clean your house, and it'll be perfect for Halloween—dusty, dingy, and filled with cobwebs.

Just say no if a zombie invites you over for lunch.

Do birds say "twig-or-tweet" on Halloween?

Try saying this three times quickly: "Overeager ogre eater."

Did you hear about the three vampires who called themselves the Three Casketeers?

How do ghouls find things on the internet?

They do Ghoul-gle searches.

What game did the skeletons like to play in the haunted house?

Bat-minton.

If you enjoyed this book, be sure to check out these hilarious titles!

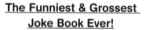